Choose a topic and start to practise writing. Each booklet has a theme to help you start to write…stories, reports, articles, letters and many more. Start collecting them now.

Guinea Pig creative writing booklets also provide extra practice for children who have completed:

- Creative Story Writing ISBN: 9780955831508
- Persuasive Writing & Argument ISBN: 9780955831515
- Information Writing ISBN: 9780955831522

They are for:

* children who are working at Key Stage 2 of the National Curriculum, levels 3-5 (in Years 5 and 6 of primary school).
* children who are working at Key Stage 3, levels 3-5 (Years 7 and 8 of Secondary School).

They provide practice for all 9-13 year olds, especially children taking 11+ examinations.

Written by Sally A Jones and Amanda C Jones

Published by GUINEA PIG EDUCATION

2 Cobs Way,
New Haw,
Addlestone,
Surrey,
KT15 3AF.

www.guineapigeducation.co.uk

Let's **learn** to *write* <u>non-fiction</u>.

When you *write non-fiction*, **<u>you may write</u>**:

- a newspaper report

- an information leaflet

- instructions

- a diary entry.

- a biography

- an autobiography

<u>You must decide</u>:

1. Who will be my target audience?

2. Who will read this writing?

3. What is the purpose of my writing?

You may be writing to inform your reader. Information writing will include **<u>facts</u>** (points that are true) and **<u>opinions</u>** (points the writer considers to be right and wants you to believe.

Use a non-fiction writing **plan** to *write* a **biography**.

<table>
<tr>
<td>

PARAGRAPH 1

- Introduce the subject or the person you're writing about.

</td>
<td>

</td>
</tr>
<tr>
<td>

PARAGRAPH 2, 3, 4...

- Make point one: the person's childhood

- Make point two: his or her adult life

- Make point three: achievements he or she is remembered for.

- Organise your writing. Write the points in a logical order as they happened.

</td>
<td>

Remember:

- Use connectives or conjunctions:

- and or but (to join compound sentences)
- or, so, if, when, while, after, before, because, unless, until, whereas, although (to join complex sentences)
- use pronouns - who, which, whose, what, that
- to link ideas use - firstly, later, therefore, on the other hand, at that moment, by this time, next, soon...

- Use linking words at the beginning of paragraphs

further more, what is more, more than this, however.

- Use a range of sentences – simple, compound and complex sentences

</td>
</tr>
<tr>
<td>

Conclusion

- comment again about the main points. As the writer, you can add your opinions saying what you think.

</td>
<td>

</td>
</tr>
</table>

Thomas Edison was one of the world's most successful inventors. Without the devices he invented, the world would not have the technology it has today.
Let's read his story:

His childhood

Thomas Edison was born on February 11th 1842, in the village of Milan, Ohio, USA. During his childhood, he developed a problem that made him partially deaf. From the start, he was a serious little boy, who didn't make friends of his own age and was content with his own company. For this reason, he only spent three months at school, because his mother home schooled him after he became known as a dunce, (a word for a stupid boy in the class).

In fact, he had a natural curiosity and was eager to learn. He loved reading and would read history books from an early age. When his family moved to a new town, he vowed to read every book in the public library. At 9 he received a book on physics, but he did not believe the experiments in it until he had tested them himself, in his science laboratory that was in the basement of his home.

His teenage years

Most children are working hard in school today at the age of twelve, but Thomas had a job as a newspaper boy on a long distance steam train. Because he enjoyed chemistry so much, he set up a laboratory in one of the back carriages. Unfortunately, the chemicals blew up, setting fire to the train so that was the end of that job.

After he saved the life of the stationmaster's baby (from being hit by a train), he found a friend who taught him the trade of telegraph operator. He soon became skilful in taking and sending messages. By fifteen years old, he was in charge of a whole office. His enquiring mind made him determined to understand how the telegraph machine worked and he experimented with a battery in his father's cellar until he understood it. Then, he invented a device called a telegraph repeater, which enabled him to handle messages that came through fast. He experimented with sending more than one message at a time.

A genius at work

Thomas's employers considered him to be a dreamy young person and were quite impatient with him, so he drifted from job to job. However, he carried on working hard on his inventions and spent all his wages on books and scientific apparatus. At the age of twenty-one, he invented a stock ticker for offices. For this, and other inventions in the office, he was paid eight thousand pounds. This is worth about three hundred forty five thousand pounds today. This meant he was able to set up a factory in Newark, New Jersey, with three hundred employees, manufacturing electrical apparatus. Here, in an atmosphere of enthusiasm, he made a lot of money. He sold more than fifty inventions, until poor health made him give up his factory. His first patent was granted in 1869, for the invention of an electric vote recorder.

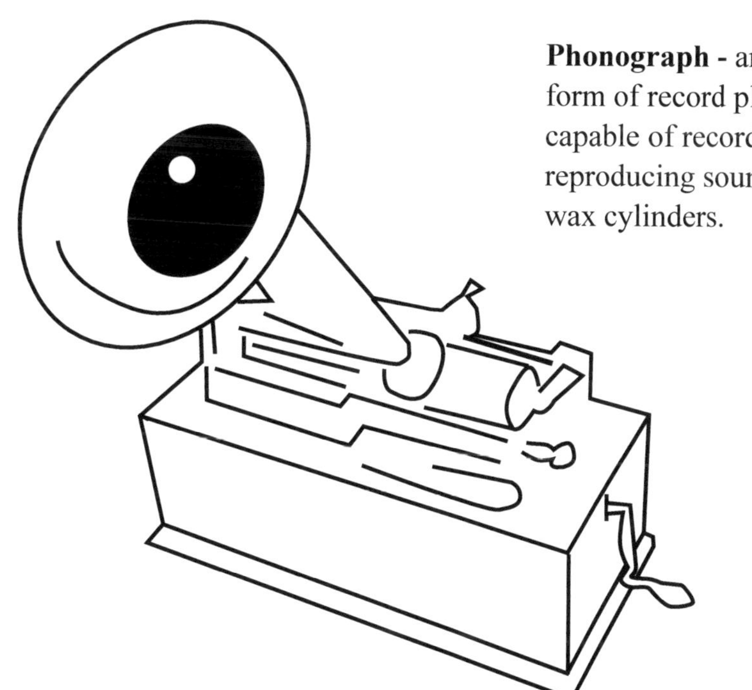

Phonograph - an early form of record player, capable of recording or reproducing sound on wax cylinders.

<u>**Self Employed**</u>

By now Thomas Edison (in his thirties) had a family and he moved them to a small house with a big laboratory. He thought nothing of working five days and nights without sleep. Most of the time, his wife and children dined alone, for the 'wizard' as he was called, was never to be disturbed. He ate when he was hungry and rested when he was tired, working eighteen to nineteen hours a day. He was as fanatical about his work as some people are about football.

His diligence (hard work) paid off. He worked on some of his inventions for years, trying to perfect them and spent a lot of money on them, using this motto: 'be sure they are needed or wanted, then go ahead'. In this way, he made more than a thousand inventions: the phonograph (an early form of record player 1878), the long distance telephone, the Edison battery, the carbon microphone used in the telephone and the kinema (a system for making moving motion picture) are a few of the inventions that owe much to Edison. He holds about 1,093 patents for new inventions.

<u>**Becoming rich and famous**</u>

In 1879, Edison and consulting electrical engineer William Hammer (building on the work of others such as Joseph Swan), invented the electric light bulb. The long lasting, incandescent electric light bulb made him rich, but cost him years and vast expense to perfect. He sent men round the world to get the right filament (you pass an electric current through the filament to make the bulb hot). In 1880, Mento Park was first illuminated, followed by a huge electric station, which lit Orange New Jersey. Edison formed the Edison Electric Light Company in 1878 in New York, with the help of financial backers.

Edison received great honours and many medals for his work. In 1915, he received the Nobel Peace Prize for physics. Wealth and fame did not take away his love of work. It has been said that the secret of his success was due to his ability to spend years of slow, patient experiment on some trivial and uninteresting problem. Edison, a genius of a thousand inventions, had unshakable optimism, a wonderful imagination and these qualities in his character distinguished him from ordinary people. He died in 1931 at the age of eighty-four years. He was famous for the words, 'Genius is one percent inspiration, ninety nine percent perspiration.'

Imagine a boy who was too busy to play, but without his inventions the world would go back in time…

Now use the story to fill in the information in the boxes.

Name: **Date of Birth:** (when he was born) **Place of birth:**	Thomas Alva Edison ....
His childhood:	• .... • By his own curiosity he taught himself. He was too busy finding out to play with other children.
His adult life:	• After inventing some office equipment, he made .... • He used the money to acquire .... until .... • Later, he bought a small house with a big laboratory for........................ .... • Here, he worked 19 hours a day, eating and resting only when .... • He had shabby work clothes and .... • He hated to be disturbed so ....

Interesting details of Thomas's teenage years:	• His favourite subject was .... • Edison started work selling newspapers on a long distance train and ....
There were no limits to his interest in science.	• He experimented with batteries in his fathers cellar until .... • He invented a telegraph repeater to allow him to .... • He loved inventing so much, that he spent all his money on ....
Electric light made him money, but it cost him a fortune to perfect as he had to send men all over the world to find the right .... **was one of the first places to have**.................	• He invented ....
Achievements:	• If his inventions were removed, the world would be .... The secret of his success was .... In 1915 he won ....

Re-read the facts about Thomas Edison's life. Then write a biography of his life. Include some information on his inventions.

ALBERT EINSTEIN	made the first air powered flight
WILLIAM SHOCKLEY	founded the apple computer and i-pod.
THE WRIGHT BROTHERS	an astronomer who discovered the galaxies
ALEXANDER GRAHAM BELL	invented the transistor (a tiny component that makes up micro chips in computers and TVs)
STEVE JOBS	showed that light was the fastest thing in the universe, with his theory of relativity (Is this still true?)
EDWIN HUBBLE	discovered that a vibrating steel strip, (called a reed) at the end of a line can vibrate a reed at the other end of the line and give out a sound – what device did he invent?
HENRY FORD	opened up a factory that produced cars cheap enough for the ordinary person to afford
JOHN BAIRD	he invented the technology that led to the television being invented

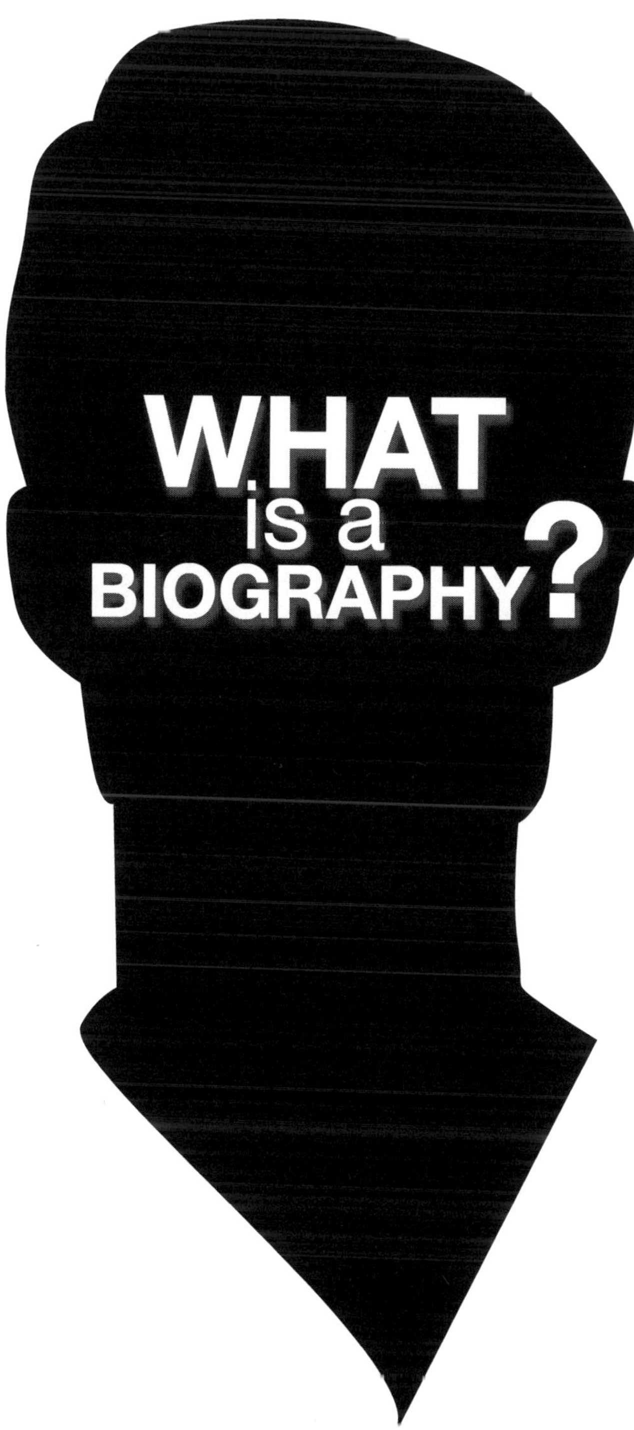

It is a **STORY** *about* someone's **LIFE.** It contains:

- **FACTS** *about* their **LIFE.**
- **EVIDENCE to** support the information.

Make a list of places where you might find evidence about someone's life:

diaries

journals

parish records

newspaper reports

photos

social networking sites

Is all evidence true?

FACTS ARE TRUE.

'Eddison was born on February 11th, 1847'.

This is true because it happened at that time.

OPINIONS might NOT be TRUE.

'Eddison was the greatest inventor of all time.'

This depends on the attitude of the writer. Opinions may be biased. For example, if the writer admires the person he is writing about, he might say:

'He worked tirelessly and selflessly on his inventions, which would change people's lives.'

If he wants to criticise him, he might say:

'He was a selfish man, who put his work before his family.'

We can get more evidence if we interview people. Choose a person you know well. Ask if you can interview them. Make a list of questions that you could ask.

Think of some headings when planning your interview – school, job, interests and achievements, for example.

Some questions only require a short answer.

- Where were you born?
- Which place did you grow up?
- Where did you go to school?
- Which friends did you have?
- Did you go to college or university?
- What was your first job?

Some questions are more open and they allow the person being interviewed to express his or her opinions.

- Do you like to buy designer clothes?
- Was it always your ambition to be a ...?
- Do you think it is important to work hard at school and get qualifications?
- What have been your biggest achievements so far?

Now write some questions of your own.

- ....?

- ....?

- ....?

- ....?

- ....?

- ....?

Use this chart, to help you plan your interview with your chosen person.

Name:	
Date of Birth:	
Place of Birth:	
Details of Life: *(married/single/do they have children)*	
Details of Childhood: *(What school did they go to?)*	
Details of Adult Life: *(Job)*	
Biggest successes and achievements:	
Quotes from the interview:	

Now write a biography of your chosen person.

Lizzie goes back into her family tree. She wants to find out about her great grandad.

Name:	Francis Wakely
Date of Birth:	24th September 1921
Place of Birth:	Warwick
Details of Life:	• Moved to Suffolk • Went to the grammar school in Ipswich • Passed his school certificate • Played the piano
Details of Childhood:	• Served in the British army in Italy during the war • Married Felicity • Had 2 daughters Sarah and Christine
Details of Adult Life:	• Worked as an electrical engineer for air traffic control at a military air base
Biggest successes and achievements:	• Received an award for long service
Died:	April 2nd 2002

Now, it is your task to write the biography of an old person in your family or one of your ancestors.

Name:	
Date of Birth:	
Place of Birth:	
Details of Life:	
Details of Childhood:	
Details of Adult Life:	
Biggest successes and achievements:	
Died:	

Imagine that you are a biographer writing about an up and coming young movie star. Make this fictional character up.

.... was born on 29th February 1994. She is the daughter of ....
.... When she was young she attended ....
By the time she was thirteen, she had already appeared in at least a dozen films, including ....
.... Despite her extraordinary career as a child actress, she is a sincere, down to earth girl who enjoys ....
.... (She learnt to read at the age of two) and ....
....

Make a list of your favourite celebrity movie stars. Research their lives (on the internet). Write a short biography about them. The following phrases will help you write your biography. Change the order to make a good structured piece of writing.

- He/She has worked with famous people like...
- The girl/boy is known for...
- He/She was born in...
- He/She appeared in...
- His/Her name is...
- His/Her films include...
- Before he/she was ten he/she was nominated for...
- He/She is very talented because...
- At the age of ten, he/she acted in...
- The schools he/she attended were...
- He/she played the part of...
- When he/she auditioned for the part, he/she was chosen out of...
- The part he/she played was...
- He/She starred in...
- His/Her latest film is...
- Besides being an actor/actress he/she is...
- At school he/she achieved...

Now write the biography you planned.

GUESS WHO? I AM?

BORN	21st April 1926
PLACE	London
PARENTS	Albert George and Elizabeth Bowes Lyon
SISTER	Princess Margaret
MARRIED	Philip, Prince of Greece and Denmark
JOB	Driver in the Women's Territorial Service in the war

Ruled England after her coronation in June 1953 |
| **ACHIEVEMENTS** | Has ruled England as sovereign for nearly sixty years.

Well loved and fulfils lots of social engagements |

BORN	30th December 1865
PLACE	Bombay India
MARRIED	Caroline and had two children
JOB	Journalist and writer of fiction and poetry
ACHIEVEMENTS	Was an immensely popular writer and poet for children and adults

Wrote the Jungle Book and the Just So stories

Received the Nobel prize for literature in 1907 |

BORN	1028
PARENTS	Illegitimate son of Robert, Duke of Normandy.
ACHIEVEMENTS	Became Duke of Normandy in 1035, aged seven. Claimed that King Edward had promised him the English throne. Won the Battle of Hastings – killing King Harold on Christmas Day 1066. He ordered a survey of Britain, which is known as the Doomsday Book and is the oldest legal document in Britain.

BORN	1757
PARENTS	Salzburg, Austria
SIBLINGS	Youngest of seven children, but five didn't survive childhood.
ACHIEVEMENTS	He was a talented genius. At the age of four, he was writing short compositions At five, he was performing on stage At the age of seven, he picked up a violin at a concert and played it perfectly, although he'd never had a lesson. Toured Europe with his father and sisters Composed many operas During his life, wrote a lot of music that we play today.

BORN	26th April 1564
PLACE	Stratford Upon Avon
PARENTS	A wool merchant and glove maker.
MARRIED	Ann Hathaway
JOB	Poet and playwright Performed plays at court
ACHIEVEMENTS	Working in theatre in London in 1592. In Kings Company in 1603. Wrote poetry, sonnets and plays, like Midsummer Nights Dream and Romeo and Juliet.

BORN	27th December, 1822
PLACE	Jura France
PARENTS	Father worked as a cleaner.
ACHIEVEMENTS	Got a PHD Taught chemistry in the university Did research on bacteria Discovered germs attack the body from outside He explained the causes of disease and developed a vaccine against rabies An institution in Paris is named after him.

BORN	1541
PLACE	Tavistock, Devon
JOB	Seaman Worked on first English slave ships
ACHIEVEMENTS	Sailed a ship called the Golden Hind Was the first Englishman to circumnavigate the globe He fought the Spanish in the American colonies Eventually he defeated them in the Spanish Armarda

BORN	September 1533
PLACE	Grccnwioh
PARENTS	Henry VIII and Anne Boleyn
CHILDHOOD	Exiled from court Imprisoned by sister Queen Mary briefly in the Tower of London
MARRIED	Never married.
DIED	1603
ACHIEVEMENTS	Succeeded to the throne in 1558 Made England a Protestant country. Expanded trade overseas Attaokod by Spanich Armarda – but united country against enemy.

Write some more biographies about famous people, for example:

- MPs and politicians (Winston Churchill)
- Historical figures (Florence Nightingale, who started a training school for nurses and served in the Crimean War as the 'lady of the lamp')
- Scientists (James Lister, who discovered antiseptic)
- Celebrities (movie stars, T.V. stars, singers) (Marilyn Monroe)
- Musicians (Beethoven)
- Sports men and women (football players, golfers, rugby players) (Eric Liddell – a famous marathon runner)
- Members of the royal family (Queen Victoria)
- Authors (Jane Austen, an eighteenth century novelist)

If you write about yourself it is called an autobiography.   Below is a piece of autobiographical writing. Vlad is going to meet a family he's never met before.

A Day In The Life Of Vlad: My Dutch Exchange

I remember that dark morning. I was woken up early by the arms of my dad shaking me. I slowly clambered out of my bed and prepared for what was going to be a very long day. As dad drove me to my school, I listened to the drumming beats of loud music, hoping it might wake me up. Dad squeezed the car into a tight parking space and we made our way towards the coach, surrounded by sleepy children, whispering parents and busy teachers.

As the coach drove down the empty motorway, the sun began to peek out from behind the hills and my classmates began to wake up and start to murmur. We were all very nervous, but also curious about the days to come. I wondered what my exchange partner would be like, whether we would get on well and if his family would welcome me. These thoughts spun around our minds and made us even more anxious.

The coach arrived on time and drove on to the ferry. Everyone got out and we followed our teachers up the spiral staircase from the car deck into the ferry's lounge. The teachers showed us the meeting point and commanded that we checked in every half an hour, but otherwise we were free to explore the boat. After two hours of shopping, eating and exploring the ferry, we arrived in Calais and the coach sped off along the motorway towards Holland.

We travelled through the French countryside, admiring the scenery through the windows of the coach. We saw brick houses with small cars parked outside and beautiful gardens with strawberry vines growing up the fences. In Belgium, we stopped off at a chocolate shop, where we purchased some sugary snacks. I had a coffee flavoured ice cream and bought some Easter eggs. We hopped back onto the coach and after waiting for some clucking chickens to clear the road, headed on towards the Dutch school, where the exchange would begin. The excitement grew and grew.

The coach driver parked outside the school and we got out, grabbed our luggage and made ourselves comfortable in the school canteen. An old lady strolled towards the microphone and called out our names in a Dutch accent. I was introduced to my exchange partner and we began to get to know each other.

I needn't have worried because Thom was a wonderful person, who was very kind and helpful. He took my bags and his family welcomed me. Their home was perfect. It had a large garden planted with flowers and the interior had modern furniture with lots of photographs on display. They even had a sweet dog, called Bo, which was obedient, playful and surprisingly quiet.

As the week went on, I got to know Thom better and better. We worked together on various activities and visited museums, such as the African Culture Museum, where we appreciated art and had a workshop on African instruments. We even had a guided tour round a Dutch town and learnt about the history of Holland.

One day, we cycled to school, where we had an art lesson. We had to draw our teachers, using charcoal. The art teacher was very impressed with my work. After this, we had a workshop on photography. In the afternoon, we cycled to a rugby field, where we played contact rugby and practised our tackles. It was good fun.

On the penultimate day of the exchange, we went to a zoo. The animals were kept in cages, which mirrored their natural habitats. In the cages, the climate and temperature were specially adapted to suit the animal's requirements, so they could live in the same conditions that they are used to in the wild. We saw flowers, fish, animals, birds and cacti. It was an interesting visit, but as we left the zoo, it began to drizzle and we got wet.

On top of that, the family also took me go carting and laser questing. I was amongst the top five winners at laser questing, but at go carting, I managed to crash into a wall and injure my leg and ribs. It was a good job I was wearing a helmet. I hope I didn't make a fool of myself. The reason I say this is because it was a bad crash. In fact, part of the wall had to be taken down to get me out.

After a week, it was time to say goodbye to our exchange partners and their families. We threw our bags on to the coach, shook hands with our exchange partners and hugged their mothers. I didn't really want to go back to England, because I was having too much fun. Would my parents mind if I stayed a few more days?

We arrived in England at around two o clock in the afternoon. I couldn't wait to see my parents again. Dragging my heavy bag off the coach, I sat down on a stone wall and waited for my mum and dad to pick me up. I had bought my mum a surprise gift on the ferry – her favourite perfume. When I saw my parents, I showed off my cheesy grin and started jumping up and down and waving my arms in the air, like I was drowning. I raced into my parents' arms, laughing, because I was so happy to see them.

I told my parents that it had been an incredible experience and I couldn't wait to do it again!

Now write an autobiography about a day in your life...

Made in the USA
Monee, IL
07 July 2026